WORLD WAR II ESPIONAGE

WORLD WAR II ESPIONAGE

Essential Library

An Imprint of Abdo Publishing
abdopublishing.com

ESSENTIAL LIBRARY OF
WORLD WAR II

BY MARCIA AMIDON LUSTED

CONTENT CONSULTANT

KRISTIE MACRAKIS
PROFESSOR OF HISTORY
GEORGIA INSTITUTE OF TECHNOLOGY

abdopublishing.com

Published by Abdo Publishing, a division of ABDO, PO Box 398166, Minneapolis, Minnesota 55439. Copyright © 2016 by Abdo Consulting Group, Inc. International copyrights reserved in all countries. No part of this book may be reproduced in any form without written permission from the publisher. Essential Library™ is a trademark and logo of Abdo Publishing.

Printed in the United States of America, North Mankato, Minnesota

052015
092015

Cover Photo: Corbis
Interior Photos: Corbis, 1, 3; Hulton-Deutsch Collection/Corbis, 6, 93, 98 (bottom); AP Images, 9, 11, 16, 19, 21, 25, 28, 33, 45, 47, 56, 63, 64, 67, 70, 74, 77, 99 (top); Carl Van Vechten/Library of Congress, 13; Farm Security Administration - Office of War Information Photograph Collection/Library of Congress, 22; Bain News Service/Library of Congress, 27; Adolph Treidler/Library of Congress, 29; Bettmann/Corbis, 30, 43, 73, 87; National Park Service, 35, 37, 38, 98 (top); FPG/Getty Images, 40; Royal Air Force Official Photographer/IWM/Getty Images, 48; APIC/Getty Images, 51; US Navy/Naval History and Heritage Command, 52; CBS Photo Archive/Getty Images, 55; Library of Congress, 58, 91, 95, 99 (bottom); US Air Force, 61; Bletchley Park Trust/SSPL/Getty Images, 78; Steven Vidler/Corbis, 81; US Marine Corps History Division, 83; Roger Viollet/Getty Images, 84; Dick DeMarsico/Library of Congress, 88; Roger Higgins/Library of Congress, 97

Editor: Nick Rebman
Series Designers: Kelsey Oseid and Maggie Villaume

Library of Congress Control Number: 2015930971

Cataloging-in-Publication Data

Lusted, Marcia Amidon.
 World War II espionage / Marcia Amidon Lusted.
  p. cm. -- (Essential library of World War II)
Includes bibliographical references and index.
ISBN 978-1-62403-797-9
1. Espionage--History--20th century--Juvenile literature. 2. Spies--History--20th century--Juvenile literature. 3. World War, 1939-1945--Secret service--Juvenile literature.   I. Title.
940.54--dc23
                                                        2015930971

CONTENTS

Allied troops wade ashore during the D-Day landings on June 6, 1944.

CHAPTER

1

★ ★

UNDER COVER AND UNDER FIRE

It was the spring of 1944, and the German army controlled France. The Allied forces were planning what would become the D-Day invasion of Normandy, France, for June of that year. One of the keys to their success would be accurate intelligence about the Germans. The Allies wanted to know about the Germans' weapons, their troop positions, and anything else that would help prepare for a successful invasion.

René Joyeuse, who was born in Switzerland, worked as a spy for the Allies. That spring, the Office of Strategic Services (OSS), a US intelligence organization, secretly sent Joyeuse to France. He parachuted into France and lived in an abandoned farmhouse where he could begin to observe and report back to the Allies on German activities. With the help of the French Resistance, a group of civilians who secretly gathered intelligence about the Germans and sabotaged their activities whenever possible, Joyeuse obtained information about a German oil refinery and an underground factory that was producing V-1 flying bombs. As a result of Joyeuse's information, both of these facilities were bombed before D-Day, making it more difficult for the Germans to provide fuel and weapons to their troops.

D-DAY

D-Day, originally code-named Operation Overlord, was the largest amphibious military operation in history. It was a risky operation, carefully planned over many months by the Allied commanders. Taking place on June 6, 1944, it involved hundreds of thousands of Allied troops invading Normandy, France—either by landing on the beaches or by parachuting in from the air. D-Day resulted in the loss of thousands of Allied and German troops, but it turned the tide of the war and helped the Allies defeat the Axis powers.

SURROUNDED

However, as Joyeuse was transmitting the locations of these German facilities to the Allies via radio, he was cut off. A powerful flashlight beam swept suddenly through the room. The Gestapo, the German secret police, had found Joyeuse and surrounded the farmhouse. Joyeuse told the Resistance fighters with him they all needed to get out quickly. He had just picked up his gun from the table when four German hand grenades came through the window. The blast threw him to the ground. Joyeuse described his experience:

We dashed into the alley and reached a small service staircase in the back of the house. We succeeded in leaving the house at the moment that the Germans entered through the garden gate.[1]

Members of the French Resistance wave as Allied troops enter the village of Quillebeuf, France, in 1944.

Joyeuse ran for a wall that separated the farm from a neighboring park, but he was unable to climb it. He told the Resistance fighters to escape on their own, and he never saw them again. Joyeuse continued fleeing as the Germans, guided by the light of flaming torches, shot at him with machine guns and rifles. He said:

They still missed me. I crossed all the tracks and came to another gate leading to the street. . . . I climbed over. At this moment, two other Germans with machine guns woke up to what was going on and fired. Luckily in climbing over the gate I had fallen flat on my face behind a small cement parapet which caused all the bullets to ricochet.[2]

Joyeuse was shot in the foot, hand, and kneecap, and he suffered several cuts and bruises. He finally crouched in a doorway, one hand on his Colt revolver and the other clutching the suicide pill given to spies in case they needed to kill

THE FRENCH RESISTANCE

In the spring of 1940, the Germans invaded France and occupied it. Charles de Gaulle, the leader of Free France, urged the French people to continue fighting against Nazi Germany. As a result of the invasion and de Gaulle's words, French citizens who were against the Germans formed several groups that together were known as the French Resistance. These groups differed in roles and in how violent they were. Some were nonviolent and published underground newspapers or anti-Nazi writing. Others, including the group known as the Maquis, intended to hurt or kill the German forces occupying their country. The Germans were ruthless in their treatment of Resistance members, torturing or killing them when they were discovered. By 1941, the British Special Operations Executive (SOE) branch of intelligence began to build relationships with the French Resistance groups. In 1943, the United States also began supporting and working with the Resistance. Eventually, all of the different groups were merged into one. During the course of the war, the Resistance committed many acts of sabotage. It also collected and passed along intelligence. Its members played an especially vital role during the preparations for D-Day.

After meeting up with American soldiers, members of the French Resistance sit down for a simple meal.

themselves. Joyeuse said, "I decided to use one or the other on myself if I were surrounded. The dragnet continued for me all night."[3]

Joyeuse did escape, even though the Germans caught and executed his Resistance colleagues. He continued to collect valuable intelligence for the Allies through the rest of the war. When the hostilities were finally over, Joyeuse moved to the United States and became a doctor. The Allies greatly appreciated his wartime services. As a result, after his death in June 2012, he was buried in Arlington National Cemetery in Virginia. This cemetery is the final resting place for many of the country's greatest heroes.

Joyeuse is an example of what most people think about when they think of spies: someone like James Bond, who is often in danger, usually shooting it out with the enemy. But while Joyeuse was definitely a valuable part of the "shadow war" of World War II—the war that took place undercover, not on the battlefields—he was only one kind of person involved in espionage during the war.

A SPY ONSTAGE

One of Paris's most exotic singers and dancers during World War II was an American, Josephine Baker. She moved to

BOND. JAMES BOND.

Author Ian Fleming was involved in espionage during World War II, working for British Naval Intelligence. He took part in the planning of Operation Mincemeat, a deception that fooled the Germans into thinking an invasion was going to take place in Greece and Sardinia rather than Sicily. Coming up with dangerous and elaborate missions was something he did well—and he also participated in an actual spy mission in the field, stealing and copying German documents. After the war, when he began writing novels about the fictional spy James Bond, he fictionalized many actual events and devices in his books, modifying them for the Cold War period.

France to appear onstage in nightclubs and was often called "Black Venus," "Black Pearl," or "Creole Goddess."[4] But Baker was much more than a flashy performer who captivated French audiences. She had been recruited by the French intelligence agency and was an undercover agent for the French Resistance.

Baker helped the Resistance in many ways. She often overheard conversations between German officers attending her performances in the nightclub and would relay any information that seemed useful to the Allies. She also exposed French officers who were actually working for the Germans. Baker was a well-known star whose presence was part of the Paris nightclub scene, and she often interacted with important people, including Japanese officials and Italian government members. She could later report back to the Allies on what she had heard from

After the war, Josephine Baker became involved in the American civil rights movement.

SCANNING THE WAVES

Allied spies had to overcome a major obstacle when sending radio messages to their commanders: the Nazi D/F (direction finding) teams. Their job was to find illegal radios being used by the Resistance and by espionage operatives. If a spy had his or her radio plugged into an electric outlet and broadcasted for more than a half hour, the Nazi D/F team could isolate that signal by turning off a city's electric current section by section until they were able to determine which area the broadcast had come from. If they turned off power to a particular section of the city and the broadcast ceased suddenly, then they had a fairly good idea the broadcast was originating in that section. Then they patrolled the streets in that particular section, using miniature listening sets, until they found the broadcast. As a result, Allied spies learned to keep their messages very brief to avoid being discovered.

them in casual conversations. Baker even went to parties in the Italian embassy and gathered information without anyone ever being suspicious of her.

Baker also traveled a great deal, visiting major cities in Europe and entertaining the troops. This gave her an opportunity to collect information and pass along messages and documents. When traveling from France to Portugal, she even smuggled information that had been written in invisible ink on the pages of her sheet music. Baker's traveling performances also provided cover for other agents. She could help them get visas by claiming they were a part of her performing company. Of course, she was also able to use her charm and appeal to help these other agents, using her "smile to end all smiles" to persuade them to help her.[5]

For her service to France during World War II, Baker was given the Croix de Guerre and the Medal of the French Resistance with Rosette, and she was named a Chevalier of the Legion of Honor, all very prestigious French awards.

IT TAKES ALL KINDS

Espionage during World War II took all kinds of people: "classic" spies such as René Joyeuse, undercover operatives such as Josephine Baker, and many others who had the access or the expertise to benefit their country. Many of these people did their jobs so well they would never be known or recognized after the war was over. Some lost their lives while serving. Others operated behind enemy lines and endured harsh conditions in concentration camps and other dangerous places, all to work for the cause of defeating the enemy.

It is hard to imagine modern governments and conflicts without espionage, intelligence operations, and other covert activities. But as World War II started in Europe and the United States realized it was likely to become involved in the war, the Americans did not have a solid intelligence organization in place. It would take the work of a president and a major general to establish an organization that still functions today.

Radio operators in Southeast Asia transmit a message, knowing the enemy is likely to

CHAPTER

★ **2** ★

WHY SPIES?

While espionage has always played an important role in American history, especially in wartime, World War II was the first time the United States found itself in need of a cohesive, organized governmental department to coordinate these activities. Espionage is a practice that includes a wide variety of activities, including spying, intercepting communications from the enemy, sabotage, and deception. According to MI5, the British intelligence agency:

> *Espionage is a process which involves human sources (agents) or technical means to obtain information which is not normally publically available. It may also involve seeking to influence decision makers and opinion-formers to benefit the interests of a foreign power.[1]*

While espionage is most important in times of war or conflict, it is used during peacetime as well, particularly between countries with uneasy or hostile relationships. Espionage is not the same thing as intelligence, however; intelligence is all of the difference types of information gathered by a government, through various methods, to help guide its decisions. Intelligence can be gathered through public or private means. Espionage comes into play when spying is necessary to gather intelligence covertly or from sources that are not available through regular means.

As the United States entered World War II, the nation needed both intelligence-gathering and espionage activities. To help the Allies plan their military maneuvers, spies and other observers could collect information about the enemy's troop movements, weapon depots, equipment, factories, and manpower. Anything that affected military operations, especially the strength of the enemy and how much resistance they might offer, was vital to planning and battle strategy. Spies could also obtain actual battle plans, often by infiltrating enemy command or going behind enemy lines. In addition, spies could feed misinformation to the enemy, giving them false intelligence about Allied strength and movement. This technique could lead the Axis armies to place their manpower in the wrong location. It could also cause Axis leaders to believe the Allied forces in

THE WAR'S BEGINNING

World War II began in Europe when German leader Adolf Hitler invaded Poland on September 1, 1939. Germany's invasion prompted the United Kingdom and France to declare war on Germany. India, Australia, New Zealand, and Canada declared war on Germany as well. In September 1940, Japan and Italy joined forces with Germany to create the Axis powers. The Soviet Union became involved in the fight against Germany in June 1941. Although the United States provided some aid to both the United Kingdom and the Soviet Union, it stayed on the sidelines until December 1941, when the Japanese attack on Pearl Harbor brought the United States into the war.

A British officer listens to two men who spent more than a week behind enemy lines and gathered information about the German military.

a particular location were weak, when in fact they were strong. Meanwhile, Axis spies were attempting to do the same thing to the Allies.

Part of gathering intelligence about the enemy was intercepting secret communication. In some cases, this involved intercepting invisible ink messages and radio messages. In other cases, it involved cracking the codes the enemy used to transmit information. Every important message was coded, and Allied spies often went on missions to capture the German or Japanese codebooks that would enable them to "crack" intercepted coded transmissions. When cracked, these messages would help in planning military strategy. Spies were not the only ones responsible for carrying out espionage, however. The personnel who worked long hours in offices to decode enemy communications were just as vital to the success of the war.

SABOTAGE

Sabotage is the act of damaging or destroying part of the enemy's infrastructure in order to disable it. During wartime, sabotage can be used to interfere with the enemy's communications. Sabotage is also carried out on industrial targets such as oil refineries and factories. In these cases, the goal is to disrupt the enemy's ability to produce weapons and equipment such as guns, tanks, and airplanes. Sabotage not only hinders the enemy's ability to support its war efforts. It also forces the enemy to take soldiers away from battle and use those troops to guard vulnerable industries and structures instead.

EYES ON THE WORLD

Espionage has many benefits in times of war, and when World War II began, espionage organizations were a vital part of many countries' governments. These governments did not just spy on governments they considered to be their enemies. They also collected intelligence on allied countries and their intelligence operatives. This practice could help identify possible double

A German arms plant burns after being set on fire by Danish saboteurs.

agents or plots that might negatively affect the country; it could also provide information that might not be readily shared between governments. Agents also spread propaganda about their governments. British spy Roald Dahl, for

American soldiers patrol a dock, on the lookout for saboteurs.

example, was sent to the United States with a partial goal of writing positive articles about the British and their involvement in the war.

When US leaders began to realize the United States might soon be involved in the war, the nation did not have intelligence departments in place. There had been spies during the American Revolution (1775–1783) and the American Civil War (1861–1865), but compared with other countries' intelligence services, the United States' services were primitive and ineffective.

In 1939, when war broke out in Europe, the United States had four separate government departments that dealt with different aspects of intelligence. The State Department gathered intelligence through its official business with other countries, or by secretly obtaining intelligence from contacts the department had established in foreign countries. The Federal Bureau of Investigation (FBI) did not actively seek to gather intelligence but sometimes acquired it anyway; this occurred when the organization investigated crimes that involved foreign people and situations. The Office of Naval Intelligence (ONI) and the War Department's Military Intelligence Division (MID) were the two military groups that gathered intelligence overseas, but they did not have enough funding or employees to function well.

The US government did not have a clear method in place for relaying intelligence

REVOLUTIONARY SPIES

Spying during the American Revolution involved invisible ink, coded letters, and code names— many of which were new and unusual methods for spying. The most famous group of spies was the Culper spy ring, a mixture of military officials and civilians who passed along information in clever ways. For example, a message might be communicated when one female spy hung clothing on her wash line in a certain way. Another piece of information might be hidden on a farm, picked up by another spy, and taken to General George Washington. One of the ring's successes took place in 1780, when it discovered the British plan to ambush French troops who were coming to aid the colonists. Because Washington was warned about it, he was able to change his plans and prevent the ambush.

from where it was gathered to the people who could best use it. Each department sent information up its own chain of command, but they did not usually share information with other departments. In addition, there was no certainty that critical information made it to the White House. In 1939, President Franklin D. Roosevelt had urged these four groups to do a better job of sharing their information, but not much had happened by 1940. As one ONI report stated, "A real undercover foreign intelligence service, equipped and able to carry on espionage, counter-intelligence, etc. does not exist."[2]

The British government, already involved in the war and equipped with a solid intelligence organization, pressured the United States to improve its intelligence system. So on July 11, 1941—five months before the attack on Pearl Harbor plunged the United States into the war—President Roosevelt created a new government agency called the Coordinator of Information (COI). The COI's mission was to collect and analyze any information that could possibly affect national security. The agency then organized and presented the information to the president and

AN UNLIKELY SPY

Roald Dahl, the author of *Charlie and the Chocolate Factory*, is a familiar name to many young readers. But long before he wrote his famous children's books, Dahl worked as a British spy during World War II. He had been a pilot until a crash resulted in severe injuries that made him unfit to fly. After the crash, he began working for British intelligence. His role was to socialize with powerful people, especially women, in the United States and use them to promote the United Kingdom. He also wrote propaganda for American newspapers. He gained support for the United Kingdom at a time when the United States was trying to stay out of the war, and he was even able to pass valuable documents to the British government.

In the days following the Japanese attack on Pearl Harbor, guards patrolled the Golden
Gate Bridge in San Francisco, California, to prevent acts of sabotage.

to any other government officials and departments that might need to know about it.

To lead the new COI, President Roosevelt chose William J. Donovan, known as "Wild Bill." Donovan was a lawyer, a former assistant US attorney general, and a World War I hero who had earned many medals and honors. He had also traveled to the United Kingdom as an official emissary for the president. In this role, he had sent back many reports on British intelligence and how the United States could improve its own intelligence.

Unfortunately, the US government's other intelligence departments did not always cooperate with the COI. After Pearl Harbor, however, when it was clear the existing intelligence networks had not seen the attack coming, the president created a new version of the COI under the authority of the Joint Chiefs of Staff. Formed on June 13, 1942, it was called the Office of Strategic Services (OSS).

CIVIL WAR SPIES

During the American Civil War, both the Union and the Confederacy needed spies to gather information. As technologies such as photography continued improving, they were put to use for spying. Confederate spies even learned how to reduce the size of messages using photography, making them small enough to conceal inside hollow metal buttons. Both sides also developed codes for conveying secret messages. In addition, balloons were used for aerial reconnaissance, enabling agents to gather information about troop movements and positions from above. Some of the most successful Civil War spies were women, as they were least likely to be suspected of espionage and could move more easily between the two sides.

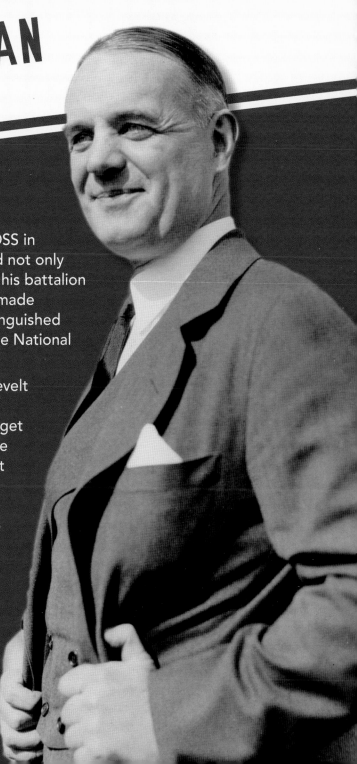

WILLIAM J. DONOVAN

1883–1959

William Donovan, nicknamed "Wild Bill," was the man President Roosevelt chose to lead the newly created OSS in 1941. Donovan served in World War I, where he earned not only the Medal of Honor but also his nickname. The men in his battalion called him "Wild Bill" because of the difficult drills he made them perform. Donovan also went on to earn the Distinguished Service Cross, the Distinguished Service Medal, and the National Security Medal.

As World War II heated up in 1940, President Roosevelt sent Donovan to the United Kingdom as an unofficial representative. Donovan spoke with British officials to get a sense of whether they would be able to withstand the forces of Nazi Germany. During this time, Donovan met with the head of the British intelligence organization and realized the United States would need a strong intelligence organization of its own. He reported these findings to Roosevelt when he returned to the United States. Donovan's part in organizing and leading the new OSS gave him another nickname: the Father of American Intelligence.

PROPAGANDA
WINNING HEARTS AND MINDS

Propaganda is the process of either helping or damaging a cause by affecting the minds and emotions of the people involved. During World War II, both the Allies and the Axis powers used propaganda to persuade people to be sympathetic to their causes. They also used propaganda to spread fear and undermine the loyalty of the enemy's forces.

Experts divide propaganda into three "colors." White propaganda comes from real, acknowledged sources such as the British Broadcasting Corporation (BBC). It consists of reporting real news, with an emphasis on positive news. Gray propaganda comes from unknown or undisclosed sources. While these sources might be spreading propaganda, they never admit to producing the broadcast. This occurred when Allied stations would broadcast jazz music and pro-American messages within Germany. Black propaganda is a broadcast that tries to hide its source. Examples include German broadcasts pretending to come from an Allied source, spreading false news to discourage Allied troops.

German guards stand in front of a movie theater during the premiere of *Triumph of the Will*, a Nazi propaganda film.

PROPAGANDA FROM THE AIR

Both the Allies and the Axis powers used balloons and aircraft to drop propaganda leaflets. These were printed sheets of paper, or even books, that spread false news or attempted to trick soldiers. Some Allied propaganda told German soldiers how to fake illnesses. Another was a fake booklet that looked like a German medical manual and listed a series of harmless symptoms that it claimed were life threatening. The booklet's creators hoped the German soldiers reading it would be distracted and stop fighting. False news reports claimed German military officials were faking their own deaths in order to desert their armies because they believed their side was losing. The Allies also printed maps showing German troops surrounded by Allied forces. All of these propaganda leaflets were attempts to dishearten German troops and decrease their effectiveness.

U. S. ARMY
OFFICIAL POSTER

SOLDIERS *without guns*

An American propaganda poster urges women to take jobs in war-related industries.

During training exercises, a man disguised as a nanny pulls a gun on a soldier.

CHAPTER
★ **3** ★

SPY SCHOOL

The United States had its new OSS. But now Donovan had a huge job: creating an espionage organization that could compete with the established organizations around the world. With very little to build on, Donovan recognized one of the most important steps would be training people to work in espionage.

Donovan needed to create a training program for spies, and he needed to do it quickly. Fortunately, he had spent time with the British intelligence organization, and he had observed their programs and training firsthand. The British had experience and their own training curriculum, so they worked with Donovan to design a school program for the United States. The goal was to train American spies, saboteurs, and people who could use guerrilla warfare tactics.

At first, the OSS recruited people through recommendations and informal contacts. The OSS was interested in people with foreign language skills, and it preferred people from middle-class backgrounds who were not affiliated with extreme political groups. People such as doctors, dentists, police officers, military veterans, radio engineers, and scientists had desirable skills for OSS work.

Sometimes the OSS even recruited people such as forgers and burglars, who were criminals but had useful and specialized skills. Eventually, the OSS developed a more formal approach to finding people for the organization. It created a series of tests and training exercises for identifying people who would be good for the OSS, as well as filtering out people who would not be appropriate. Those who passed the tests were then sent on to training camps where they would learn the particular skills they needed for the roles they would carry out for the OSS.

The OSS built several special training camps, most of which were in the eastern United States. The most famous one, known as Camp X, was in Canada. Even though it was just outside Toronto, getting to the camp was a training exercise in itself because its location was top secret. Frank Devlin, who was one of the first Americans to train there, recalled his trip:

SPY ORGANIZATION

The OSS was divided into several departments, each with a specific purpose. Research & Analysis (R&A) analyzed intelligence; Research & Development (R&D) developed special weapons and equipment; Morale Operations (MO) created propaganda; Maritime Units (MU) transported personnel and also sponsored naval sabotage and reconnaissance; X-2 worked in counterespionage; Secret Intelligence (SI) managed agents who were secretly gathering intelligence in the field; Special Operations (SO) specialized in sabotage and guerrilla warfare; and Operational Groups were made up of highly trained operatives who spoke foreign languages and were part of elite commando teams.

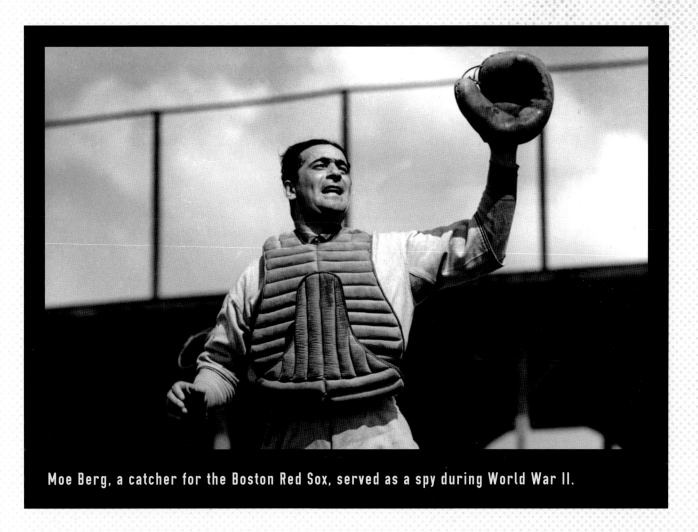

Moe Berg, a catcher for the Boston Red Sox, served as a spy during World War II.

I was given a set of orders that read like a spook book. "Have civilian clothes. Take train such and such to Penn Station New York and get a train to Toronto Canada. Go to Hotel and there you will find a message with a number. That number indicates a license on the vehicle you will take and it will be at the west entrance of the hotel."[1]

In the OSS training camps, agents learned about hand-to-hand fighting and the use of weapons and explosives. They also learned about "dirtier" types of fighting, such as "gutter fighting," which combined martial arts and street fighting. One OSS officer, Dan Fairbairn, even taught his trainees how to roll an ordinary newspaper into a lethal dagger. Agents also learned about sabotage, receiving training on demolitions, explosives, and the best ways to destroy structures.

A WALK IN THE PARK

During World War II, the peaceful park in Prince William Forest near Dumfries, Virginia, became a secret training camp for OSS forces. The park was a training ground for thousands of military men and everyday citizens for more than four years. They practiced skills such as intercepting radio signals and doing translations, as well as setting up transmitters and receivers. They were also taught survival skills. Similar activities took place at what is now Camp David, the official presidential retreat in Maryland.

Spies needed to learn other skills as well. They had to learn the basic vocabulary of espionage, such as the differences between various types of agents and how to recruit agents from the enemy to work as double agents for the Allies. Spies also had to learn about photography, secret writing, surveillance, reading a compass, and ciphers and codes. In addition, they learned how to use dead drops, prearranged locations where spies could leave information or collect instructions or equipment.

OSS recruits also learned more specialized skills if they were to work in a specific location or department. Many recruits were put into Operational Groups and given relevant training. For some, this included parachute training

in different types of terrain, such as rivers or mountains. For others, it meant maritime training that included submarines, inflatable rafts, and the use of one-man underwater propelled rafts. These vehicles would later be used to secretly enter enemy territory, where the agents could collect intelligence or perform sabotage on ships and harbors.

HIDDEN IN ORDINARY PLACES

One of the essential parts of passing along intelligence and secret messages was to develop hiding places the enemy would never suspect. An agent would never carry sensitive information in a pocket or purse. Instead, spies developed a wide variety of creative ways to conceal their information. A message might be rolled up and inserted into the handlebars of a bicycle, placed in the base of a statue, tucked inside a toilet paper roll, concealed within a hollow coin, enclosed inside a toy, or even hidden in an artificial eye.

OUT IN THE FIELD

Once OSS agents had completed their camp training, they were often required to participate in mock missions that took place in the real world. Because most OSS training centers were near Washington, DC, many of the training scenarios took place in the nearby cities of Baltimore, Maryland, and Philadelphia, Pennsylvania.

The first stage of training was usually simple, such as practicing sabotage by breaking into a power plant and leaving a note saying "This is a bomb."[2] The second stage of training was more intense; it often required the agent to assume another identity and carry out a mock mission to acquire intelligence. The exercises were so realistic that some agents were caught by local authorities or the FBI and sent to jail. In some cases, it could take days before the FBI contacted the OSS to verify the agents really belonged to the OSS and could be released.

New recruits at a camp in Virginia receive instruction on setting up a radio antenna.

Trainees practice sending and receiving messages in Morse code.

Toward the end of training, OSS agents were invited to a party that was supposedly given for relaxation and fun. In reality, it was a test to see if they would relax and give up their cover. The party included alcoholic drinks, stories, and teasing between teachers and students. By loosening up the trainees, observers at the party could learn a great deal about "practical intelligence, emotional stability, and motivation and propaganda skills," according to a document describing the parties' true purpose.[3]

Overall, OSS training taught agents about leadership, creative thinking, being confident, and taking decisive action. Most important, the training taught the agents they were expected to win. Through their own skills, agents were capable of success—but some clever gadgets would certainly help.

THE MURDER MYSTERY TEST

To test their investigative skills and ability to make inferences, OSS trainees had to take the Murder Mystery Test. Agents were given a fake copy of a local newspaper with a story that said a woman's body had been found several miles from a village. More clues and eyewitness accounts were provided. Each agent was told that he or she was the only one investigating the murder and was responsible for solving it. At the end of the test, the training staff would assess each agent's conclusions and declare one the winner.

Spies hid information in a variety of places, including artificial eyeballs.

CHAPTER

4

★ ★

THE RIGHT TOOLS FOR THE JOB

When most people think about spies, especially fictional spies, they think of all the interesting gadgets, equipment, and devices spies use. This equipment is not all fiction; spies during World War II had many amazing tools and gadgets. The British secret services created some of these devices, while the OSS developed others.

Because agents found themselves in such a wide variety of situations, their equipment had to be adaptable to individual needs. The equipment had to be easy to conceal, but it was equally important for it to be durable. After all, a device might not be used for months or even years at a time, but it still had to function flawlessly when it was needed.

EYE SPY

Collecting intelligence on the enemy required several important tools. Some tools, such as cameras, helped agents take pictures of the information they found and store it on film.

As photographic technology developed from the middle of the 1800s, cameras became increasingly important spy tools. During World War II, it was vital that agents be able to take photographs of places such as airfields, factories, supply depots, and other facilities that could have an effect on enemy war plans. Most important, agents needed to take pictures of secret written communications such as office memos, war plans, and blueprints.

Engineers developed many kinds of special cameras for agents. Some cameras were small enough to be concealed in wristwatches, neckties, buttons, jewelry, umbrella handles, cigarette packets, books, and even under an agent's clothing. Digital photography did not yet exist during World War II, and that meant all cameras used film. As a result, many cameras had tiny film cassettes that were easy to load, unload, and conceal. Other cameras could be carried in a purse, and the agent would simply point her purse at the object she wanted to photograph.

IN DISGUISE

Sometimes an agent's best way to monitor enemy agents and avoid being captured was to disguise himself or herself. Using makeup, wigs, fake facial hair, wrinkle cream, false teeth, and other methods, an agent could appear to be anyone from a farmer to a nightclub singer. This was particularly helpful if an agent was already known to the enemy, as a disguise would enable the agent to avoid being recognized.

A spy demonstrates how she uses a camera concealed beneath her skirt.

One of the most ingenious inventions involved the creation of quiet cameras. In regular cameras, the film had to be wound by hand to advance to the next photo. This process was noisy and drew attention to the camera user. Therefore, engineers invented "robot" cameras with spring-driven motors that advanced the film automatically and silently. The only drawback was that the agent could not use a viewfinder to see if he or she was aiming the camera at the object. Consequently, agents had to learn by instinct how to position a hidden camera correctly.

MICRODOTS

One method for secretly transmitting messages, images, or documents was the use of microdots. A microdot was a reduced image of a photograph, and it could be read only with a special magnifying viewer. The dots were as small as 1 millimeter in width.[1] They could be hidden almost anywhere, including in jewelry, in the seams of clothing, and under toenails. Microdots could even be embedded in the edge of a postcard; they were retrieved with a tool that slit the edge of the card and extracted the dot.

Some cameras were developed specifically for photographing documents quickly. Agents often had only moments to make copies of documents before they were discovered. Regular cameras required time and skill to take good photographs of documents, but copy cameras made the process faster and created higher quality photos. Some copy cameras fit inside briefcases, and others could be assembled quickly from small boxes.

Photographed documents could be reduced in size and made into microdots, which were tiny photographs the size of a period. Agents could easily hide microdots and later enlarge them to retrieve the information. Dusko Popov, a double agent who told the Germans he was working for them but was actually working on behalf of the Allies, showed a German microdot to FBI head J. Edgar Hoover in 1941. Hoover was very impressed; the

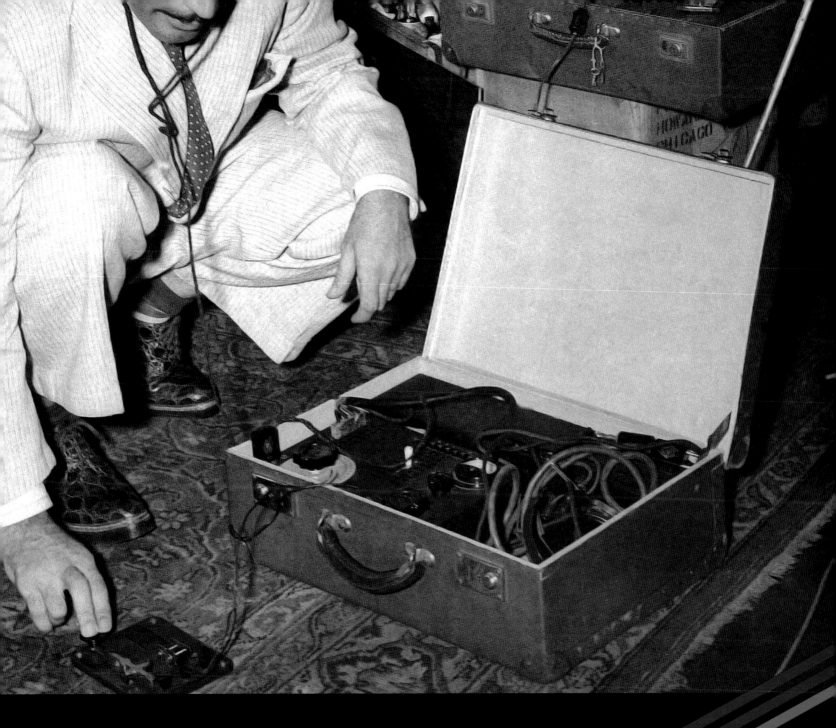

A man examines a radio found when authorities uncovered a German spy ring.

US government had not been aware of this technology. By the end of the war, however, the FBI had created an even smaller version of the microdot than the one the Germans were using.[2]

EAVESDROPPING

Specific tools were designed to help agents gain access to enemy communications without being detected. Agents sometimes had to listen in on conversations secretly, either in person or by installing bugging devices.

If an agent wanted to record a meeting secretly, he or she sometimes used a special pen that contained a recording device. Later, engineers developed books with microphones and transmitters concealed in their spines. There were also special shoes with transmitters concealed in the heel.

LOCKS WITHOUT KEYS

Agents often had to break into locked places, so they needed devices for picking locks and copying keys. A special key-casting kit allowed agents to make a copy of a key in the field by making an impression in clay with an existing key.

SPIES IN THE SKIES

Carrier pigeons were valuable messengers during World War II. These birds instinctively return to their home lofts no matter where they are released. Therefore, agents who were in locations where radio transmissions were impossible could fasten a message to a pigeon. After releasing the bird, the agent knew it would return to headquarters with its information. Pigeons could fly as far as 600 miles (965 km) from where they were released to reach their home loft.[3] While pigeons would eventually be replaced by modern communications technology, they were such reliable message carriers during World War II that most of their messages never had to be encrypted.

German spies used a rubber boat to make their way into the United Kingdom in 1941.

The impression could then be used as a mold to make a temporary copy key, which could be duplicated later.

Agents also learned how to pick locks at spy school. To open a regular key lock, they used a picking tool and a tension wrench, which could be inserted into the lock and manipulated like a key.

Members of the Royal Air Force study film taken by an aerial camera

When agents were captured or imprisoned, they needed tools to help them escape. These tools, known as escape and evasion aids, included knife blades, compasses, and maps. They were usually concealed inside everyday objects that did not arouse the suspicion of enemy captors. For example, some agents carried special playing cards that could be soaked in water to remove the outer layer and reveal a portion of a map. Each card held a different map section and, when assembled like a puzzle, formed a master escape map. Other escape tools, such as files and compasses, were concealed in Monopoly game boards. Humanitarian organizations provided these games to people in prisoner of war camps. Other agents carried a hairbrush with a removable section that revealed a secret compartment containing a miniature saw, a compass, and a map printed on tissue-thin paper. Coins and steel shoe heels could have blades concealed inside. Pens and pipes could contain compasses. For female agents, buttons, lipstick tubes, high-heeled shoes, and even corsets contained hidden compartments for weapons.

CIPHERS

Intelligence organizations have created many ingenious devices for making messages unintelligible to everyone but their intended recipients. German diplomats used the Kryha Cipher machine, which used polyalphabetic substitution. This meant each letter was substituted with a different letter, and the recipient needed a matching machine to decode the message. The M-94 was a cipher device used until 1943. It consisted of a series of rotating disks of letters placed around a cylinder. The US Army used the Converter M-209, which had a series of rotors to encrypt and decrypt military messages. Once coded, a message could be sent by radio and then decoded by a matching machine on the other end.

EXPLODING MUFFINS AND MANURE

Some devices were designed to commit sabotage. "Aunt Jemima" was an explosive flour that could be baked into bread or muffins and easily transported across enemy lines.[4] Explosives were also hidden in objects that looked like lumps of coal or the manure of horses or mules. The coal could be placed in a locomotive's coal car and would explode when shoveled into the train's boiler. The fake manure could be left on roads that enemy vehicles were likely to use.

There were also special ways to conceal weapons for defense. The Stinger was a three-inch (8 cm) pen that actually concealed a .22-caliber gun. Guns were also hidden in tobacco pipes and umbrellas. Pistols could be made small enough to conceal in a cigarette pack. Guns were also concealed in belts, carried up an agent's sleeve, or disguised as cigars or pens. Other weapons looked like ordinary walking sticks, umbrellas, or newspapers, but they produced poison gas or shot poison pellets from hidden compartments.

THE LAST RESORT

Agents sometimes had to make difficult decisions. Could they keep from revealing secrets even when in great pain? Or was it better to die for their country in order to keep their information safe? In hopeless situations such as these, agents needed methods for taking their own lives.

Therefore, many agents had L pills, or lethal pills, which could be used if they were facing interrogation or torture. This way, the agents would be unable to reveal any information. The pills were coated with rubber. If an agent bit down on one and swallowed the contents, the result was instant death. If an agent

Fighter pilots received escape kits, which contained lethal pills.

swallowed the pill without chewing, it would pass harmlessly through the body. Some OSS agents in World War II had to resort to using their L pills to keep from betraying the Allied cause.

Before the attack on Pearl Harbor, the Japanese gathered as much information as

CHAPTER
★ **5** ★

THE MISSIONS

Many countries involved in World War II had their own espionage activities. Both the Allies and the Axis powers sent their agents on missions of spying, sabotage, and misinformation.

PREPARING FOR PEARL HARBOR

Before their successful attack on Pearl Harbor on December 7, 1941, the Japanese had to gather the necessary intelligence to conduct the attack. By monitoring the US Pacific Fleet's radio traffic, they were able to discover how many ships, and what kinds of ships, were in Pearl Harbor. They learned the radio call signs for many US ships and could track their movements. They also tracked the flights of US aircraft around the harbor and learned that most reconnaissance flights went to the west and south of the Hawaiian Islands. This information made the Japanese realize a successful attack could be launched from the north.

The Japanese also had a spy network, called Organization F, with one agent operating out of the Japanese consulate in Honolulu. This agent, Takeo Yoshikawa, sent information to Japan by taking photographs of ships and writing down their movements. He made many of his observations from teahouses and restaurants that overlooked the harbor. Yoshikawa also observed the security measures the US military was using at nearby bases. He even studied the harbor itself by using a glass-bottomed boat and by swimming. In this way, Japanese military planners learned Pearl Harbor was shallow. Therefore, they adjusted their torpedoes so they would destroy the US ships rather than just sinking them; after all, a ship that sunk in shallow waters could be raised and repaired. Yoshikawa also reported on the way US ships were moored in double rows. This information helped the Japanese plan the attack in a way that would do maximum damage.

JAPANESE INTELLIGENCE

The Japanese forces had their own intelligence organizations. The Tokko was a special bureau of the Tokyo police force charged with counterintelligence within the country. The military police, called the Kempei Tai, controlled counterintelligence activities in territories occupied by the Japanese. And Organization F, a network of Japanese agents stationed throughout Southeast Asia, was responsible for acquiring information that led to the attack on Pearl Harbor, Hawaii. The Japanese also ran the TO network out of Spain, which gathered intelligence on US shipping.

OPERATION GREIF

The Japanese were not the only ones with active espionage networks. The Germans had an expert commando and spy named Otto Skorzeny, and in 1944 he succeeded in infiltrating the Allied lines with his own agents. Skorzeny's mission was to disrupt

Takeo Yoshikawa returned to Japan in 1942 as part of a prisoner exchange.

Allied communications and bring down the morale of the troops. In Operation Greif, he handpicked a small group of German soldiers who spoke fluent English. He provided them with fake US Army documents, gave them American uniforms that had been taken from captured soldiers, and sent them behind Allied lines.

Skorzeny's soldiers managed to send US tanks and convoys down the wrong road, destroy ammunition dumps, and even destroy telephone lines and change road signs. None of these activities were hugely disastrous for the Allied troops, but they caused fear, suspicion, and confusion.

As soon as US soldiers realized they had been fooled by Germans pretending to be Americans, they began questioning every soldier who came through their checkpoints. They asked questions about

Otto Skorzeny took part in many operations during World War II.

baseball and American popular culture, hoping to trap any Germans who would not know these details. Many real American soldiers were temporarily detained. The few Germans who were caught fed the Allies fake intelligence about a planned Nazi attempt to assassinate General Dwight D. Eisenhower in Paris. The threat was convincing enough that General Eisenhower was briefly put under house arrest for his own protection.

SABOTAGE ON SKIS

Some missions, while very successful, never received a great deal of attention. One of these was a sabotage mission known as Operation Gunnerside. In February 1943, the Germans controlled the Norsk Hydro Vemork plant in Norway. This plant was the only facility in the world that produced "heavy water," a form of water in which the regular hydrogen atoms are replaced with an

THE SOE

The British had a secret volunteer fighting force during World War II: the Special Operations Executive (SOE). Their mission was to carry out sabotage and subversion behind enemy lines. The people the SOE recruited and trained were from many different parts of society and included chefs, electricians, journalists, and the daughter of a car salesman. They were taken to a remote country mansion in England and trained in skills such as how to disguise themselves, how to derail a train, how to pick the locks on handcuffs, and even how to kill with their bare hands. SOE workshops were also responsible for creating some of the most ingenious spy devices, such as pistols hidden in cigarettes, a fake tree trunk that concealed a radio, and camel manure that held enough explosives to blow the tires off an enemy vehicle. The SOE carried out hundreds of successful missions during World War II.

DWIGHT D. EISENHOWER

1890–1969

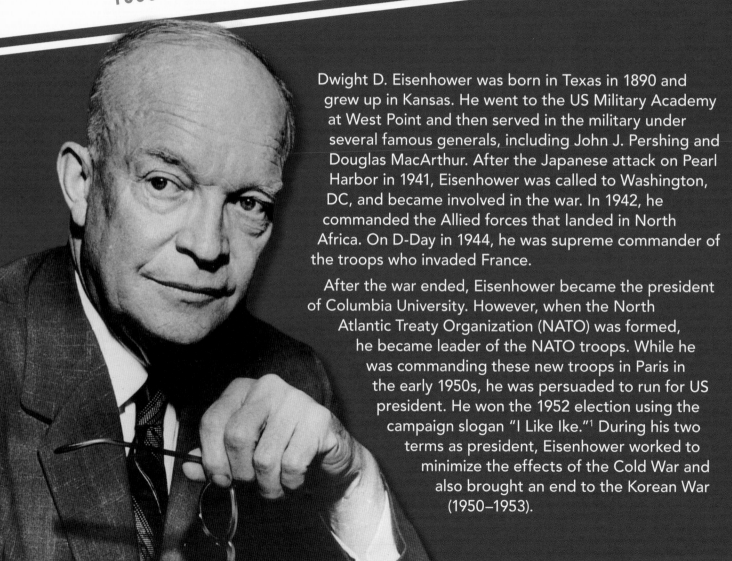

Dwight D. Eisenhower was born in Texas in 1890 and grew up in Kansas. He went to the US Military Academy at West Point and then served in the military under several famous generals, including John J. Pershing and Douglas MacArthur. After the Japanese attack on Pearl Harbor in 1941, Eisenhower was called to Washington, DC, and became involved in the war. In 1942, he commanded the Allied forces that landed in North Africa. On D-Day in 1944, he was supreme commander of the troops who invaded France.

After the war ended, Eisenhower became the president of Columbia University. However, when the North Atlantic Treaty Organization (NATO) was formed, he became leader of the NATO troops. While he was commanding these new troops in Paris in the early 1950s, he was persuaded to run for US president. He won the 1952 election using the campaign slogan "I Like Ike."[1] During his two terms as president, Eisenhower worked to minimize the effects of the Cold War and also brought an end to the Korean War (1950–1953).

isotope called deuterium. Heavy water was used as a coolant and was therefore critical to the development of atomic weapons. Because the Germans controlled this plant, they had made significant progress with their atomic research. This greatly worried the Allies, who were desperate to prevent the Germans from developing an atomic bomb.

On the night of February 27, 1943, a group of Norwegian exiles who had been living in England and received training from the British parachuted into a snow-covered pasture near the plant. They skied to the plant site, went down into a gorge, crossed an icy stream, and then climbed up to the plant. Avoiding German sentries and minefields, the Norwegians entered the plant through a cable duct. Once inside, they planted explosives in the rooms where the heavy water was stored. After the men escaped, the bombs detonated, destroying the plant and delaying the Germans' progress with atomic development by at least six months.

Operation Gunnerside would not be the last Norwegian act of sabotage. In 1944, a ship attempting to carry a large supply of heavy water to Germany was bombed and sank.

OPERATION MINCEMEAT

One of the war's most successful campaigns of intelligence and deception was carried out off the coast of Spain, a country that stayed neutral during the war. On April 30, 1943, a body was found floating in the water; it was partially decomposed, wearing the uniform of a British Royal Marine. Even more intriguing, the dead man had an important-looking briefcase chained to his wrist. The body was reported to the Spanish authorities, and the Germans convinced the Spaniards to let them examine the briefcase. After photographing the contents, the Germans put everything back into the briefcase and made it look as though it had never been opened.

The briefcase contained a letter discussing secret Allied plans for an invasion of Sardinia and Greece in the next few weeks. The Germans had stumbled on a major intelligence windfall—or so they thought. In reality, the entire incident, from the body to the invasion plans, had been staged. As part of Operation Mincemeat, British intelligence had dressed the body of a recently deceased homeless man and given him a false identity. To make his identity seem real, they filled his pockets with fake letters from his girlfriend, along with real ticket stubs from a London theater. After filling his briefcase with fake documents that had been made to look like top-secret communications, they set the body adrift off the Spanish coast.

A few days later, British officials contacted Spain's government and asked for the briefcase to be returned. The idea was to make it seem as though the deceased person had been an important courier. The British received the briefcase

UP, UP, AND AWAY

One of the sabotage techniques Japanese intelligence employed against the United States was the use of balloons. These hot air balloons, which carried explosive devices, were launched from Japan toward the US mainland and were mostly intended to start forest fires. Of the thousands of balloons launched between 1944 and 1945, the wind carried approximately 350 of them to the United States.[2] On May 5, 1945, a balloon killed a pregnant woman and five children. These were the only World War II deaths on the US mainland caused by an enemy attack.

two weeks later, and intelligence experts could tell it had been opened.

Operation Mincemeat was successful. In fact, the British achieved more than they had expected, because the Germans not only believed the deception but also thought the British did not realize the Germans had intercepted the information. As a result, the Germans diverted some of their troops and tank divisions to Greece, which meant they were taken by surprise when the Allies invaded Sicily instead.

These are just a very few of the many espionage missions and operations carried out during World War II. Some have become well known to historians, while others were quietly forgotten. And while some spies also became famous for their actions, others lived—and often died—anonymously, their valuable contributions to winning the war forever unknown.

A Japanese balloon could carry more than 30 pounds (14 kg) of explosives.

INTERNMENT CAMPS
PRISONERS IN THEIR OWN COUNTRY

As much as espionage and intelligence were beneficial in shortening the war and saving lives, there was also a dark side to these activities. The West Coast of the United States was home to many people who were Japanese Americans or of Japanese ancestry. After the attack on Pearl Harbor, people across the United States panicked, thinking everyone of Japanese ancestry was a possible spy or saboteur.

As a result of this new fear, President Roosevelt signed Executive Order 9066 in February 1942. This order moved 120,000 people of Japanese descent to internment camps with guard towers and barbed-wire fences.[3] These camps were located in isolated areas in Arizona, Idaho, Utah, and Wyoming.

People were forced to leave their homes and businesses, and they were allowed to bring very few personal items with them. Many families put all of their household goods into storage, while others sold their homes and businesses. Most of those who relocated were Nisei, or people born in the United States whose parents had emigrated from Japan. Even veterans of World War I who had fought for the United States were forced to relocate.

The internment lasted for the duration of World War II. But even after the order was repealed, many people could not return home because of hostility against them. Thousands moved to other parts of the country. In 1988, the US Congress attempted to apologize for the relocation order by awarding $20,000 to each surviving internee.[4]

People of Japanese descent prepare to leave San Francisco for an internment camp.

A Danish saboteur places an explosive device on a railroad track likely to be used by the

DOUBLE AGENTS AND SABOTEURS

A double agent is a spy who pretends to be working for one country while actually working for another. For example, a double agent might have been hired by the Germans to spy on the Allies, but secretly, his loyalty was with the Allies. He might send inside information about the Germans' plans back to the Allies, or he might give the Germans false information about the Allies' plans.

Other double agents turned against the organization or country that had first recruited them and worked for another agency, all while making the first agency believe their loyalty had not changed. It was a very risky role to play, but skilled agents were able to pull it off.

Double agents usually turned from one side to the other because they believed in the cause of the new agency they were spying for.

Another reason for turning included the possibility of personal gain. In some cases, agents who had been uncovered were afraid of being captured or killed, and offering to work as a double agent was the only way to stay alive.

The British set up an organization called the Double Cross Committee, also known as the XX. Its purpose was to control German spies in the United Kingdom without their leaders in Germany ever being aware. The XX set up several large networks of fake German spies or double agents who appeared to be

IRENA SENDLER

Irena Sendler was a social worker in Poland when World War II broke out. Part of her job was to help the poor and homeless people in Warsaw. But when the Germans forced 400,000 Jews to live in the sealed-off Warsaw Ghetto, Sendler could no longer assist Jewish families.[1] Conditions were terrible inside the ghetto, and Sendler managed to obtain a permit as a sanitation inspector, allowing her to enter the ghetto on "inspections." She helped smuggle many Jews out of the ghetto and away to safety. Later, she used her contacts with orphanages to smuggle Jewish children, many of whose parents had been sent to the Treblinka extermination camp, out of the ghetto. Sendler used methods such as hiding children in trunks or suitcases, smuggling them out through sewer pipes and other secret underground passages, or having them pretend to be sick and taking them out in an ambulance, often with more children hidden under the stretchers. Sendler wrote notes on thin tissue paper to record each child's family and where the child was initially taken—all written in code and buried in glass bottles and jars to be recovered later. The Germans arrested Sendler in 1943 and sentenced her to death, but underground activists bribed officials to release her and pretend she had been executed. She spent the rest of the war in hiding.

loyal to Germany even though they were being controlled by British intelligence. While 13 German spies were executed in the United Kingdom during the war, approximately 40 more cooperated with the British and served as double agents.[2]

One of the XX's greatest successes was British double agent Eddie Chapman. Before the war, Chapman had been a thief and explosives expert. In the early 1940s, he was serving a prison sentence on the British island of Jersey, located in the English Channel. While in prison, Chapman offered his services to the Abwehr, the German secret service. The Germans had recently occupied the Channel Islands, giving Chapman access to German officials. The Abwehr was desperate for better intelligence from the United Kingdom. They also liked the fact that Chapman had experience

Eddie Chapman lied to the Germans, saying their V-1 bombs were hitting densely populated central London.

with explosives from his criminal safe-cracking days. In addition, Chapman still had connections with the UK criminal underworld, which had the potential to provide Germany with more spies.

The Abwehr trained Chapman and then sent him on his first mission into the United Kingdom. However, Chapman immediately reported to the British—and after interrogating him, the British agreed to let him work as a double agent. Code-named Zigzag, Chapman performed many important missions for the British. He so thoroughly fooled the Germans that they awarded him their highest honor, the Iron Cross, for a sabotage attack on a British airplane factory that never actually took place.

THE ABWEHR

From 1921 to 1944, the German intelligence organization was known as the Abwehr, which is the German word for "defense." It was given that name because the Allies insisted, after World War I, that the Germans use intelligence activities only for their own defense. The Abwehr's original duties included monitoring radio traffic and ciphers, reconnaissance, and counterespionage. However, in January 1935, Wilhelm Canaris took over the leadership of the Abwehr and reorganized the agency into three divisions: the controlling Central Division; the Foreign Branch, which evaluated most of the intelligence gathered by the other divisions; and the Abwehr I, II, and III, which collected intelligence, committed sabotage, and performed counterintelligence. Hitler dissolved the Abwehr in 1944, and most of its duties were taken over by the SS, the Nazi security service. The Nazis executed Canaris in April 1945, shortly before the end of the war.

OPERATION TORCH

In November 1942, the American and British militaries worked on their first joint mission. Known as Operation Torch, it was a plan to land Allied troops in French North Africa. This area, which the Germans did not yet fully control, would provide the Allies with an excellent way to invade Axis territory in the rest of North Africa and then move into Europe from a new direction. The plan called for Allied forces to invade Morocco and Algeria; the French government, which was collaborating with the Nazis, controlled these countries. The invasion succeeded, and Allied forces ultimately pushed into Tunisia, where they defeated the Germans' Afrika Korps.

In addition to its military success, Operation Torch also enabled a British agent to gain credibility as a double agent. Juan Pujol García was a Spanish citizen who had become part of the German intelligence organization by claiming to be in favor of the Nazis. But Pujol actually supported the Allies, and he offered to work for the British as a double agent. Code-named Garbo, Pujol built an elaborate network of 27 subagents who supposedly worked with him to deliver information to the Germans.[3] In reality, Pujol made up all these subagents and their life stories.

During Operation Torch, Pujol fed the Germans what was actually true information about the Allied landing plans. However, Pujol timed his information to arrive too late for the Germans to do anything about it. Even so, Pujol managed to gain the Germans' trust—and when the Allies began planning the vital D-Day landings in Normandy, France, Pujol created another deception to mislead the Germans. Through a fake plan called Operation Fortitude, Pujol

Allied troops land in North Africa as part of Operation Torch in November 1942.

helped convince the Germans the Allied invasion would be in Pas de Calais, France. Pujol's part in Operation Fortitude helped draw many of the German forces away from the area of the actual landings.

DESTRUCTION BEHIND THE SCENES

People who were adept at sabotage were often invisible, meaning they worked in secret and were not always officially connected to military or intelligence organizations. However, they had usually been trained by and were unofficially connected to these same organizations. This made it possible for a government to train saboteurs and yet say truthfully that the agents were not officially working for a certain intelligence or military operation.

Sabotage caused actual damage, such as the destruction of factories, roads, and railroad lines, and it also caused low morale among troops. The fear of not knowing who or what was causing damage was difficult for soldiers to handle because there was no visible enemy to fight against.

Saboteurs received special training in how to build bombs; how best to blow up bridges, tunnels, or rail lines; and how to communicate using secret codes. Some saboteurs were also double agents, which enabled them to gain access to enemy installations. Others were experts at sneaking into facilities undetected.

Although the US mainland was far from the battlefields of Europe and the Pacific, a German operation called Operation Pastorius nearly succeeded in causing significant sabotage on US soil. In 1942, Allied forces were rapidly destroying German tanks, airplanes, and guns; meanwhile, the United States was increasing its production of such equipment. Hitler believed the war would be won by the army that was best supplied with planes, tanks, guns, and ships. Therefore, he would need to destroy American factories to ensure a German victory.

The Abwehr planned Operation Pastorius as a way to commit this sabotage. The Nazi intelligence organization trained eight men to disguise themselves as Americans and cause destruction in American factories. In preparation, the saboteurs learned American slang and memorized facts about American sports teams, politics, and movie stars.

In June 1942, four of the men landed in New York, and four more landed in Florida. Their plan was to blow up railway lines and factories that made aluminum; these acts would disrupt American war production. All eight men successfully made their way into the United States and probably would have succeeded in at least some of their planned sabotage, but on June 19, 1942, the leader of the group, George John Dasch, revealed the plot to the FBI. No one is exactly sure why Dasch betrayed the Germans, but his actions resulted in the arrest of all eight saboteurs. The men were sentenced to death, and six died in the electric chair. However, two of the

SPECIAL STAMPS

Members of the French Resistance often used the mail to tell other members when meetings were taking place. The Germans knew about this, however, and they began sending fake letters to people they suspected of being Resistance members. Then, if a person came to a "meeting" the Germans had set up, he or she would be arrested. As a result, British intelligence created fake French stamps to be placed on envelopes. These stamps looked almost exactly like real ones, but they included a tiny difference only Resistance members would know about. For example, a stamp featuring a picture of a person's face might have an extra shadow or a slightly changed facial feature. If the Resistance member saw the secret marking on the stamp, he or she knew the letter was real and not a German trap.

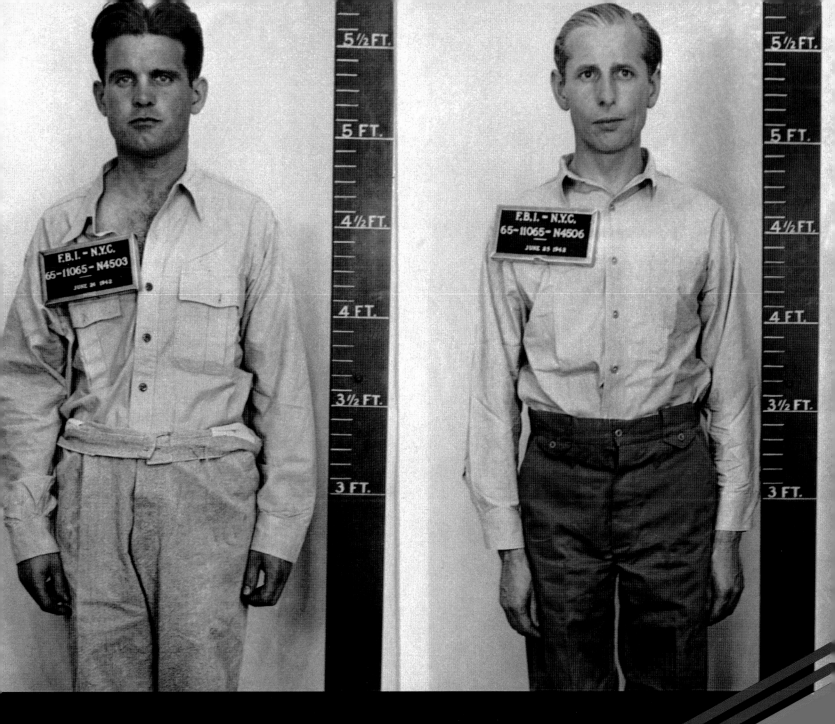

Two German saboteurs pose for booking photographs after being arrested by the FBI.

A German plane burns after being damaged by saboteurs.

men, including Dasch, had their sentences reduced. They were granted clemency in 1948 and deported to Germany after serving less than six years of their sentences.[4]

The Allies had their own methods of sabotage. The British had a special school for saboteurs, where agents received training in explosives, unarmed combat, and demolition. One of the Allies' biggest successes took place in September 1943 against the Japanese forces in Singapore. Known as Operation Jaywick, it was one of the most daring and successful sabotage missions of World War II. Fifteen British and Australian soldiers used a captured Japanese fishing boat, the *Krait*, and disguised themselves as Malaysians by staining their skin a darker color. They sailed the *Krait* into Singapore's harbor, and then several teams, each consisting of two or three of the men, were off-loaded from the boat and climbed into canoes. They stealthily attached limpet mines to the hulls of several Japanese transport ships and managed to slip away before the mines exploded. Seven Japanese ships sank.[5]

RESISTING

Resistance movements, which arose in every country occupied by the Axis powers, were made up of civilians who worked together to overthrow the enemy and its leaders. Members committed sabotage, passed along intelligence, and assisted Allied agents as much as possible. They were uniquely suited to operate

LIMPET MINES

One of the most effective ways to sabotage ships was by using limpet mines. These were waterproof bombs that were fastened to a ship's hull using magnets. They were positioned by using a placing rod, which was a rod that could be extended long enough to place the limpet mine well below water level, where it would not be seen. Typically, an agent in a small boat would quietly approach the ship to place the mine. Limpet mines had time-delay fuses to allow the person placing the mine to get away before the mine exploded. Limpet mines were capable of blowing a 25-square-foot (2.3 sq m) hole in a ship's hull, which resulted in significant damage or even sinking.[6]

undercover, as they were not officially part of any country's military forces and lived in zones occupied by the enemy.

Resistance groups published and distributed illegal newsletters to let the public know about what was really taking place. They gathered crucial information about enemy movements. They often rescued Allied pilots who had been shot down behind enemy lines, sheltering them secretly and helping them escape back to their forces. Resistance members also helped Jewish people who were being persecuted by the Germans, hiding them and helping them escape. They committed acts of sabotage by bombing bridges and roads. They rendered enemy vehicles useless by pouring sugar into gas tanks and adding sand to the grease on railroad car wheels.

The French Resistance was an enormous help to the Allies before the invasion of Normandy on D-Day, and the Yugoslavian Resistance actually drove the Germans out of their country. Even Germany itself had a small resistance movement of people who did not follow Hitler. Resistance members in any country operated at a terrible risk and were often shot. German forces were also known to round up groups of civilians and execute them as a warning to resistance members.

German soldiers capture a group of resistance fighters in Yugoslavia.

CHAPTER
★ 7 ★

CODES, DUMMIES, AND DECEPTIONS

Much of the intelligence gathering and espionage that took place during World War II relied on secret messages. Agents had to be able to transmit information to their superiors without the enemy understanding the messages' contents. Agents also made great efforts to intercept and decipher any messages the enemy passed among themselves. For this, the world of espionage relied on code makers, code breakers, and invisible ink.

WHAT DOES IT SAY?

Leaders on both sides of the war operated on the assumption that every message would be intercepted by the enemy. Therefore, information passed among the Axis and Allied forces had to be coded, or else it could be easily utilized by the other side. Some members of intelligence organizations were especially skilled at figuring out codes.

The Germans devised one of the war's most famous coding machines: the Enigma. The British were able to decipher it thanks to a team of 10,000 code breakers who worked on it at a country estate called Bletchley Park.[1] This team included academics, chess masters, crossword puzzle experts, artists, and language specialists—all of whom had skills that might help crack the Enigma.

The Enigma machine looked like a typewriter but used a series of rotors that continually changed after each letter was typed. At first, only another Enigma machine could decipher the code. In 1943, the Bletchley Park code breakers managed to build a code-breaking machine called the Colossus, which deciphered

IS IT A SHIP . . . OR AN ISLAND?

During the Battle of the Java Sea in February 1942, the Japanese destroyed almost an entire fleet of Allied ships. Only four Dutch warships survived, and their crews hoped to escape to Australia. But with Japanese planes patrolling the skies, it was unlikely the ships could travel far without being sunk.

Ultimately, three ships were destroyed. The fourth, a minesweeper called the *Abraham Crijnssen*, was disguised and made the trip safely. The crew cut down trees from nearby islands and used them to make the ship look like the canopy of a jungle from above. The ship resembled an island from the air—but islands do not move, so they could travel only by night. During the day they stayed anchored in one place. The Japanese never noticed the ship's antennae or that it was in a different place every night. Eventually, the *Abraham Crijnssen* made it safely to Australia.

The German military started using Enigma machines in the 1920s. Other countries continued using the machines after World War II ended.

not only Enigma codes but thousands of others as well. The Germans never realized the Enigma had been cracked, and they used it throughout the war.

The United States developed its own unique code to use in radio transmissions—one that the Germans and the Japanese were never able to break. They utilized Navajo Native Americans, who have a complex language with word meanings that depend on tone and inflection. In the 1940s, the language had not yet been written down, which made it even harder for the enemy to understand. The United States employed native Navajo speakers as radiomen, transmitting coded messages based on Navajo words. Approximately 400 men were trained as "code talkers," sending secure messages the Japanese could not crack.[2] One expert code breaker said, "It sounded like gibberish. We couldn't even transcribe it, much less crack it."[3] During the Battle of Iwo Jima alone, six Navajo code talkers sent more than 800 messages securely.[4] Their valuable contribution was kept secret until 1968, when the code talkers finally received awards for their service.

IS IT REAL?

Fooling the enemy was another key aspect of espionage during World War II. This required more than agents and double agents; it often required carpenters, painters, and many other logistical aspects of the military. Small deceptions included operations such as Operation Mincemeat, in which the Allies convinced the Germans that a dead body was actually an important Allied officer carrying secret documents. But much bigger deceptions took place during the war, many of which concerned the Normandy invasions on D-Day.

Two Navajo men send radio messages in their native language.

British soldiers move an inflatable rubber decoy to a new location.

The Allies knew it was of the utmost importance to keep D-Day a secret for as long as possible. So they created an elaborate plan, called Operation Fortitude South, to make the Germans think the Allied invasion of Europe was going to take place in Pas de Calais, not Normandy. The Allies wanted to convince the Germans they were building up an army that would cross the English Channel in a completely different area from where the actual invasion would take place.

To achieve this, the Allies invented a fictitious army, known as the First United States Army Group (FUSAG). They even invented fake unit badges for this army, which were featured in an issue of *National Geographic* magazine.

To further support the ruse, the Allies created physical signs of FUSAG, including mock airfields with inflatable rubber tanks and planes, harbors filled with fake landing craft, and large encampments of tents that were actually empty. The Allies also had a special broadcasting unit that drove up and down the southern coast of England, transmitting sounds that seemed like the noise of an army. The intricate preparations of Operation Fortitude South paid off: the Germans fell for the deception. On June 6, 1944, when the real Allied troops came ashore at Normandy, 19 German army divisions were waiting at Pas de Calais, far from the real landing site.[5]

GHOST ARMY

The Twenty-Third Headquarters Special Troops, also known as the Ghost Army, tricked the German forces with false information about Allied battle plans. The Ghost Army was made up of four units, each with a specific purpose. The 244th Signal Company developed and used fake radio traffic and sent fake messages. The 3132nd Signal Service Company specialized in tricking the enemy with sound. They used a mobile recording studio to record the various sounds military equipment and personnel made, and then they broadcast those sounds to fool the Germans into thinking a real army was nearby. The 603rd Engineer Camouflage Battalion built and set up camouflage and dummy equipment, such as fake tanks, trucks, airplanes, and guns made from rubber and wood. Finally, the 406th Engineer Security Company was made up of fighting troops who protected the deception artists from the enemy and lent a hand to heavy construction projects.

INVISIBLE INK

During World War II, especially before the widespread use of microdot technology, agents often used invisible ink to write messages that could not be easily revealed. Many invisible inks were made from substances such as fruit juices, milk, vinegar, or even urine. These fluids could not be seen under normal circumstances but would darken and become visible when they were heated.

Agents could write messages in these substances on the pages of an innocent-looking book, and when the message reached its destination, the receiver would simply warm the pages to read the message. Another advantage to these substances was that they were easy to get. The Germans had their own invisible ink made from quinine, a substance from a tree used to treat malaria. One Abwehr agent had a small bag of quinine rolled up and hidden inside a filling in his tooth. All he had to do was roll the quinine between his fingers and create a tiny invisible ink pencil—but he had to visit a dentist to remove the filling before he could write his message.[6]

DECOYS

Allied deceptions and decoys may have fooled the Germans, but they used their own tricks as well. They concealed rivers and bridges by covering them with camouflage nets. Then, using straw mats, they built fake bridges over other rivers to divert the Allies miles away from the real bridges. They also covered railroad tracks with straw mats to make them look like roads. However, the Germans were not as successful in creating decoy airfields. The Allies quickly realized they were not real when repeated photographs showed the airplanes on the fake runways never moved.

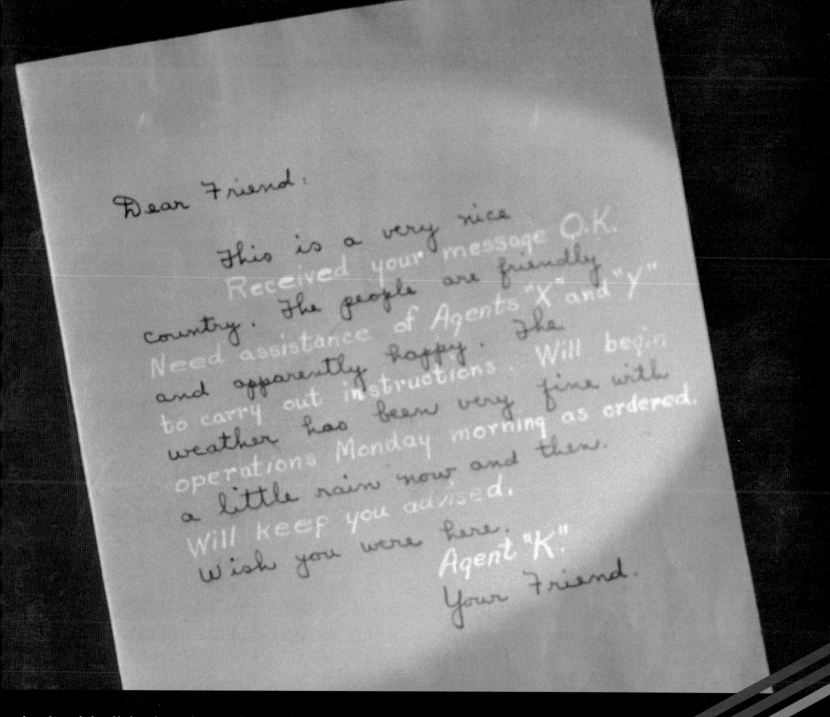

An ultraviolet light shows how an innocent-looking letter can actually contain a secret message written in invisible ink.

A huge crowd gathers in New York City to celebrate the end of the war in 1945.

WINNING THE WAR

The work of spies, double agents, resistance members, intelligence gatherers, code breakers, and many others—known and unknown—helped save countless lives and shorten the conflict. By gathering intelligence about the movements and strength of the Axis armies, the Allies were able to plan accordingly and often minimize the impact of those forces. The tremendous amount of espionage that took place in the planning of D-Day helped the invasion succeed and enabled the Allies to make their final push into Germany. The OSS and its personnel made huge contributions to the Allies' victory, despite the fact that the agency had not even existed at the beginning of the war. And British agents pioneered many techniques that would become standard spy craft.

THE MANHATTAN PROJECT

In 1939, the Allies learned that German physicists had split the atom and may have been on their way to developing an atomic bomb. Scientists Albert Einstein and Enrico Fermi contacted President Roosevelt, urging him to develop a US atomic research program. This program, approved in October 1941, was eventually code-named the Manhattan Project. Research took place in Oak Ridge, Tennessee, and Hanford, Washington, and ultimately at an assembly plant in Los Alamos, New Mexico. The Manhattan Project employed 120,000 Americans but required absolute secrecy from the Germans and Japanese—so only a handful of people knew what the project was really about.[2] The project culminated with the first successful atomic bomb detonation in Los Alamos on July 16, 1945.

AFTER THE WAR

After World War II, as the Soviet Union gained power and the Cold War began to unfold, US spies started gathering intelligence on the Communist nation's activities. This spying had its origins in the Manhattan Project, the Allies' program to develop an atomic bomb. Espionage was a way of life during the Manhattan Project, and the United States wanted to keep information about the atomic bomb from reaching the Soviet Union. However, Soviet spies were able to breach the security at the Manhattan Project in Los Alamos, New Mexico, and other important locations, sending information about the bomb back to the Soviet Union.

The Soviet Union was very successful at using spies and sources in the United States who were willing to share atomic secrets. These spies enabled the Soviet Union to develop its own atomic bomb by August 1949, which was 12 to 18 months sooner than it might have achieved this goal without the spies' help.[1] The first bomb the Soviet Union tested was virtually identical to the one tested by the United States four years earlier.

A mushroom cloud forms during a nuclear weapons test in the late 1940s

US intelligence was aware that Soviet agents had infiltrated the project. Not only were they trying to steal secrets; the Soviets were targeting physicists and scientists to kidnap for their own research purposes. American agents worked tirelessly to run intelligence missions against the Soviets, with help from unexpected sources. Some Germans were willing to assist in foiling Soviet plans, since they hated and feared the Soviets more than the Americans. The Germans would often provide information to US agents, such as the names of the next German scientists targeted for kidnapping. Dick Cutler, an American station chief in Berlin, Germany, remembers:

> [The Germans] would give us names of [the Soviets'] next targets. I would send the name of the next target to Washington and they went to the Manhattan Project and asked, "Does this German know enough to be important?" . . . If he wasn't you'd let the kidnapping proceed since you didn't want to let them know there was a mole in their operation.[3]

If a scientist was of great importance to atomic knowledge, the United States and its allies would attempt to foil the kidnapping.

KLAUS FUCHS

Klaus Fuchs, a scientist who helped develop the atomic bomb, was arrested in 1950 for passing atomic secrets to the Soviet Union. His arrest led to the discovery of an entire ring of spies who were working for the Soviets and passing along information about atomic research. Fuchs was British and had been brought to the United States in 1943 to work on the Manhattan Project. He was discovered as a spy because a series of decoded Soviet messages named him as a Soviet agent. Soviet leaders denied Fuchs had ever spied for them. Even so, Fuchs's arrest was one of the first indications that the Soviet Union had been actively spying on the Manhattan Project over an extended period of time.

Klaus Fuchs spent nine years in prison after being found guilty of spying.

The Soviet Union constructed a huge intelligence network surrounding the Manhattan Project. Most members of this network were spies and informants with Communist sympathies who volunteered their services simply because they believed in the Soviet cause.

VENONA

In February 1943, the US Army Signal Intelligence Service began a secret program called Venona. Its mission was to examine and, if possible, make use of coded diplomatic communications from the Soviet Union. Dozens of language teachers and professors from all over the United States were recruited to help decode and sort thousands of Soviet diplomatic telegrams. Some of these messages dealt with Soviet espionage concerning the secrets of the US atomic bomb program. The Venona project showed American leaders just how comprehensive and in-depth Soviet espionage activities had been in the United States and how long they had been taking place.

BECOMING THE CIA

When the war ended in September 1945, the OSS, along with many other agencies and departments, was abolished. American leaders believed the organization was no longer necessary because the nation was no longer at war. Therefore, the organization's functions were transferred to the State Department and the War Department. But with the growing Cold War threats, President Harry S. Truman soon realized there was a real need for an organization whose only job was intelligence.

Truman signed the National Security Act of 1947, which established the Central Intelligence Agency (CIA). According to the CIA, the act "charged the CIA with coordinating the nation's intelligence activities."[4] With this act, many of the techniques and structures developed by the OSS were formalized into a new intelligence organization for the postwar United States.

HARRY S. TRUMAN

1884–1972

Harry S. Truman was born in Missouri in 1884. He made a living as a farmer until 1917, when he went to France to serve in World War I. After the war, he was active in the Democratic Party and eventually became a senator. In 1944, he was nominated as Franklin D. Roosevelt's running mate and became vice president in January 1945. He had only 82 days in this role before Roosevelt's death on April 12 made him president. He assumed the presidency at a difficult time, when World War II was still raging. When Truman learned Roosevelt had died and he was now president, he told reporters, "I felt like the moon, the stars, and all the planets had fallen on me."[5]

Truman made the decision to drop two atomic bombs on Japan in August 1945. Truman had not even known about the existence of the Manhattan Project and the development of the bomb until after Roosevelt's death.

After the war, Truman supported the creation of the United Nations, a political organization dedicated to international peace and security. He also supported the Marshall Plan, which helped the countries of Europe recover economically from World War II. Truman died in 1972 and is buried in Missouri.

THE ROSENBERGS

In 1951, Julius and Ethel Rosenberg were convicted of conspiring to pass US atomic secrets to the Soviets. Two years later, they were executed in New York. The Rosenbergs had been implicated by Ethel's brother David Greenglass. Greenglass himself had confessed to passing secrets to the Soviets, but he was not executed.

Many people protested that executing the Rosenbergs was an unusually harsh sentence. However, President Dwight D. Eisenhower said,

I can only say that, by immeasurably increasing the chances of atomic war, the Rosenbergs may have condemned to death tens of millions of innocent people all over the world. The execution of two human beings is a grave matter. But even graver is the thought of the millions of dead whose deaths may be directly attributable to what these spies have done.[8]

A LASTING LEGACY

During World War II, intelligence agencies developed a modern approach to spying, with a commitment to using every weapon and type of information available. This legacy is still evident in the way the CIA operates today. As one CIA agent said, referring to the war on terror and the methods used in Afghanistan and Iraq, "What we are doing is all OSS."[6]

While some World War II spies have become famous and recognizable, many others who made vital contributions to the war will never be known or honored. Others were quietly forgotten after their deaths and as the memory of the war receded. But their contributions were every bit as important as those of soldiers fighting on the front lines. When OSS head William J. Donovan died in 1959, President Dwight D. Eisenhower said, "We have lost the last hero."[7]

Julius and Ethel Rosenberg sit outside the courtroom after being found guilty of spying.

TIMELINE

1939

World War II breaks out in Europe.

July 11, 1941

President Franklin D. Roosevelt creates the office of the Coordinator of Information (COI).

October 1941

Roosevelt approves a US atomic research program, which later becomes known as the Manhattan Project.

June 13, 1942

The COI becomes the Office of Strategic Services (OSS); training camps are established.

September 1943

In Operation Jaywick, Allied saboteurs disguise themselves as Malaysian fishermen and destroy several Japanese ships.

June 6, 1944

Allied troops successfully land in Normandy, France, and begin a second front against the Germans.

April 12, 1945

Franklin D. Roosevelt dies, and Harry S. Truman is sworn in as president.

May 5, 1945

A Japanese balloon bomb kills six people in the United States.

June 19, 1942

George John Dasch reveals a German sabotage plot to the FBI, making Operation Pastorius a failure.

November 1942

As part of Operation Torch, US and British troops successfully land in North Africa and push into Tunisia.

February 1943

In Operation Gunnerside, a group of Norwegian saboteurs destroy a plant.

April 30, 1943

In Operation Mincemeat, the British convince the Germans that the Allies will invade Greece instead of Sicily.

July 16, 1945

The first atomic bomb is detonated, and Soviet spies working on the program inform the Soviet Union.

September 1945

The OSS is officially disbanded.

1947

The National Security Act of 1947 establishes the Central Intelligence Agency.

August 1949

The Soviet Union detonates its first atomic bomb.

ESSENTIAL FACTS

KEY PLAYERS

- Franklin D. Roosevelt is the president of the United States during most of World War II.

- William "Wild Bill" Donovan is the head of the Office of Strategic Services.

- Juan Pujol is a double agent who supplies the Germans with false information.

KEY STATISTICS

- The French Resistance has an estimated 400,000 members during World War II.

- The OSS employs more than 13,000 people, approximately 2,000 of whom work as agents in the field.

- Thirteen German spies are executed in the United Kingdom during the war; approximately 40 cooperate with the British and serve as double agents.

KEY TECHNOLOGIES

Many new types of equipment are developed for spying and gathering intelligence, including photography, cryptography, concealment, weapons, explosives, and escape and evasion devices.

IMPACT ON THE WAR

Espionage and intelligence gathering reduce the duration of World War II by months or even years, saving hundreds of thousands of civilian and military lives.

QUOTE

"I was given a set of orders that read like a spook book. 'Have civilian clothes. Take train such and such to Penn Station New York and get a train to Toronto Canada. Go to Hotel and there you will find a message with a number. That number indicates a license on the vehicle you will take and it will be at the west entrance of the hotel.'"

—*Frank Devlin describing how he got to Camp X for spy training*

GLOSSARY

AFFILIATED
Officially attached or connected to an organization or group.

BUGGING DEVICE
A hidden microphone that enables people to secretly listen to a conversation.

COHESIVE
Working or fitting together well.

COLLABORATE
To work on a project jointly, or to cooperate with the enemy.

COVERT
Secret, not openly acknowledged or displayed.

DEMOLITION
To intentionally destroy, ruin, blow up, or tear down a building or structure.

ENCRYPT
To convert information into a cipher or code to prevent unauthorized access.

GUERRILLA
Warfare carried out in irregular ways, such as using sabotage, staging surprise raids, or fighting using unusual methods.

INFILTRATE
To gain access to a place or organization gradually in order to obtain secret information.

INTELLIGENCE
Information that is of military or political value.

ISOTOPE
One of the forms in which an atom can occur.

OPERATIVE
A person who is engaged or skilled in some kind of work.

ROTOR
The rotating or spinning part of a machine.

SURVEILLANCE
Close observation or watch kept over something or someone.

ADDITIONAL RESOURCES

SELECTED BIBLIOGRAPHY

Melton, H. Keith. *The Ultimate Spy Book*. New York: DK, 1996. Print.

O'Donnell, Patrick K. *Operatives, Spies, and Saboteurs: The Unknown Story of the Men and Women of WWII's OSS*. New York: Free Press, 2004. Print.

Pearson, Judith L. *The Wolves at the Door: The True Story of America's Greatest Female Spy*. Guilford, CT: Lyons, 2005. Print.

FURTHER READINGS

Atwood, Kathryn J. *Women Heroes of World War II: 26 Stories of Espionage, Sabotage, Resistance, and Rescue*. Chicago: Chicago Review, 2011. Print.

Coleman, Janet Wyman. *Secrets, Lies, Gizmos, and Spies: A History of Spies and Espionage*. New York: Abrams, 2006. Print.

Samuels, Charlie. *World War II Sourcebook: Spying and Security*. Redding, CT: Brown Bear, 2012. Print.

WEBSITES

To learn more about Essential Library of World War II, visit **booklinks.abdopublishing.com**. These links are routinely monitored and updated to provide the most current information available.

PLACES TO VISIT

International Spy Museum
800 F Street NW
Washington, DC 20004
202-393-7798
http://www.spymuseum.org
Featuring hundreds of artifacts and devices, this museum provides visitors with an interactive look at the history of espionage.

National Cryptologic Museum
8290 Colony Seven Road
Annapolis Junction, MD 20701
301-688-5849
http://www.nsa.gov/about/cryptologic_heritage/museum
With fascinating exhibits on code making and code breaking, this museum is operated by the National Security Agency.

SOURCE NOTES

CHAPTER 1. UNDER COVER AND UNDER FIRE

1. Patrick K. O'Donnell. *Operatives, Spies, and Saboteurs: The Unknown Story of the Men and Women of WWII's OSS.* New York: Free Press, 2004. Print. ix.

2. Ibid. x.

3. Ibid.

4. "Josephine Baker (1906–1975)." *National Women's History Museum.* National Women's History Museum, n.d. Web. 7 Apr. 2015.

5. Ibid.

CHAPTER 2. WHY SPIES?

1. "What Is Espionage?" *Security Service MI5.* Security Service MI5, n.d. Web. 7 Apr. 2015.

2. Patrick K. O'Donnell. *Operatives, Spies, and Saboteurs: The Unknown Story of the Men and Women of WWII's OSS.* New York: Free Press, 2004. Print. xii–xiii.

CHAPTER 3. SPY SCHOOL

1. Patrick K. O'Donnell. *Operatives, Spies, and Saboteurs: The Unknown Story of the Men and Women of WWII's OSS.* New York: Free Press, 2004. Print. 2.

2. Ibid. 10.

3. Ibid. 15.

CHAPTER 4. THE RIGHT TOOLS FOR THE JOB

1. H. Keith Melton. *The Ultimate Spy Book.* New York: DK, 1996. Print. 126.

2. Kristie Macrakis. *Prisoners, Lovers, and Spies: The Story of Invisible Ink from Herodotus to al-Qaeda.* New Haven, CT: Yale UP, 2014. Print. 198–212.

3. "Pigeons of War." America in WWII. 310 Publishing, n.d. Web. 7 Apr. 2015.

4. Patrick K. O'Donnell. *Operatives, Spies, and Saboteurs: The Unknown Story of the Men and Women of WWII's OSS.* New York: Free Press, 2004. Print. 17–19.

SOURCE NOTES
CONTINUED

CHAPTER 5. THE MISSIONS

1. "Dwight D. Eisenhower." *White House*. White House, n.d. Web. 7 Apr. 2015.

2. "5 Attacks on US Soil During World War II." *History. com*. A&E Television Networks, 23 Oct. 2012. Web. 7 Apr. 2015.

3. "Japanese–American Relocation." *History.com*. A&E Television Networks, n.d. Web. 7 Apr. 2015.

4. "$20,000, Apology Voted for WWII Japanese Internees: Bill Ready for Reagan Signature." *Los Angeles Times*. Los Angeles Times, 4 Aug. 1988. Web. 7 Apr. 2015.

CHAPTER 6. DOUBLE AGENTS AND SABOTEURS

1. "Smuggling Children out of the Ghetto." *Yad Vashem*. Yad Vashem, n.d. Web. 7 Apr. 2015.

2. "Double Cross – MI5 in World War Two." *British Broadcasting Corporation*. British Broadcasting Corporation, 17 Feb. 2011. Web. 7 Apr. 2015.

3. "Agent Garbo." *Security Service MI5*. Security Service MI5, n.d. Web. 7 Apr. 2015.

4. "George John Dasch and the Nazi Saboteurs." *Federal Bureau of Investigation*. Federal Bureau of Investigation, n.d. Web. 7 Apr. 2015.

5. "The Jaywick Operation." *British Broadcasting Corporation*. British Broadcasting Corporation, 15 Oct. 2014. Web. 7 Apr. 2015.

6. Patrick K. O'Donnell. *Operatives, Spies, and Saboteurs: The Unknown Story of the Men and Women of WWII's OSS*. New York: Free Press, 2004. Print. 128.

CHAPTER 7. CODES, DUMMIES, AND DECEPTIONS

1. "Bletchley Park Names 'Secret' World War II Codebreakers." *British Broadcasting Corporation.* British Broadcasting Corporation, 3 Oct. 2013. Web. 7 Apr. 2015.

2. "Chester Nez, Last of WWII's Original Navajo Code Talkers, Dies at 93." *Los Angeles Times.* Los Angeles Times, 4 Jun. 2014. Web. 7 Apr. 2015.

3. Brad Melton and Dean Smith, eds. *Arizona Goes to War: The Home Front and the Front Lines During World War II.* Tucson: U of Arizona P, 2003. Print. 81.

4. Ibid.

5. "Normandy." *US Army Center of Military History.* US Army. 3 Oct. 2003. Web. 7 Apr. 2015.

6. Kristie Macrakis. *Prisoners, Lovers, and Spies: The Story of Invisible Ink from Herodotus to al-Qaeda.* New Haven, CT: Yale UP, 2014. Print. 230–231.

CHAPTER 8. WINNING THE WAR

1. "Espionage and the Manhattan Project." *The Manhattan Project: An Interactive History.* US Department of Energy, n.d. Web. 7 Apr. 2015.

2. "51f. The Manhattan Project." *USHistory.org.* USHistory.org, n.d. Web. 7 Apr. 2015.

3. Patrick K. O'Donnell. *Operatives, Spies, and Saboteurs: The Unknown Story of the Men and Women of WWII's OSS.* New York: Free Press, 2004. Print. 308–309.

4. "History of the CIA." *Central Intelligence Agency.* Central Intelligence Agency, n.d. Web. 7 Apr. 2015.

5. "Harry S. Truman." *White House.* White House, n.d. Web. 7 Apr. 2015.

6. Patrick K. O'Donnell. *Operatives, Spies, and Saboteurs: The Unknown Story of the Men and Women of WWII's OSS.* New York: Free Press, 2004. Print. 313.

7. Ibid. 314.

8. "Rosenbergs Executed." *History.com.* A&E Television Networks, n.d. Web. 7 Apr. 2015.

INDEX

ABOUT THE AUTHOR

Marcia Amidon Lusted is the author of more than 100 books and 500 magazine articles for young readers. She is also an editor for the Cricket Media magazine group. She lives in New Hampshire.